the
ROCK & ROLL ALPHABET

Featuring photographs from the Chuck Boyd Photo Collection

www.chuckboydgalleries.com

Written and compiled by Jeffrey Schwartz

Dedicated to my parents, Stuart and Darlene,
for raising me in a home filled with music.

For more information on Chuck Boyd and the photographic images in this book,
please visit us online at www.chuckboydgalleries.com.

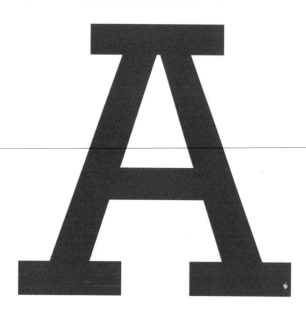

is for **A**retha, oft referred to as the Queen...

B

is for The **B**eatles in their 'Yellow Submarine'.

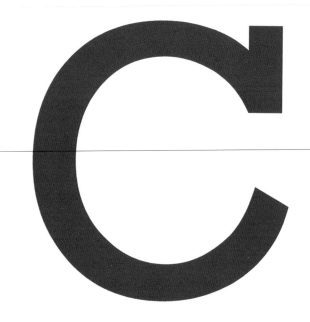

is for **C**ream and the British
blues invasion...

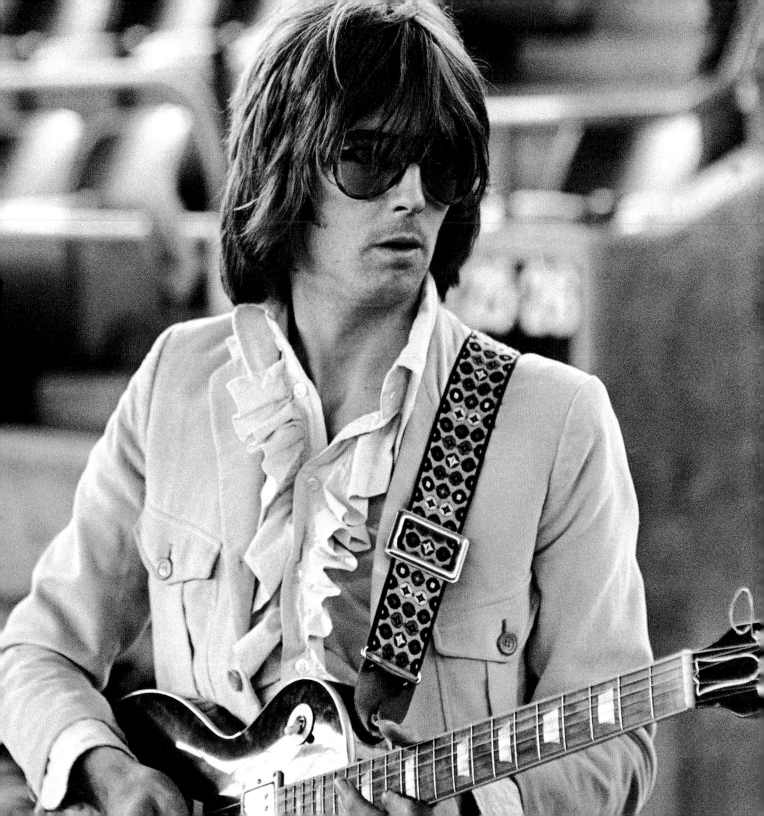

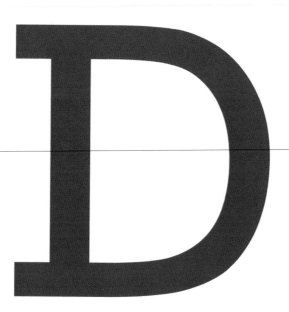

is for The **D**oors and their sonic exploration.

is for **E**lton John tickling the keys...

is for **F**leetwood Mac's vocal harmonies.

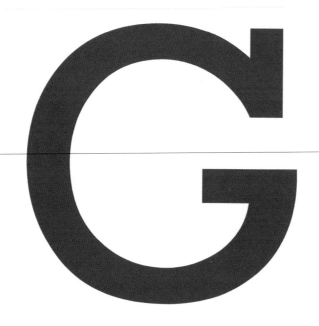

is for the **G**rateful Dead, a band
that loved to jam...

is for The **H**ollies who sang for 'Carrie-Anne'.

is for **I**ke & Tina 'Rollin' Down the River'...

J

is for **J**ames Brown, whose 'Cold Sweat' made us shiver.

K

is for **K**ISS, a sight to see on stage...

the
ROCK & ROLL ALPHABET

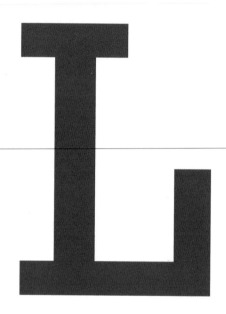

is for **L**ed Zeppelin and the songs of Plant and Page.

M

is for **M**arvin Gaye, 'Oh Mercy, Mercy, Me'...

N

is for **N**eil Young's haunting melodies.

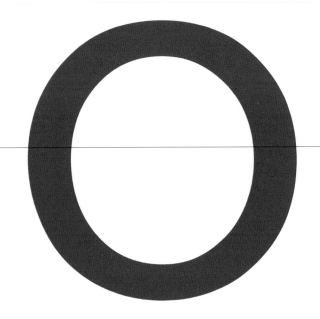

is for **O**zzy, or 'Iron Man' to you...

P

is for **P**eter Frampton; 'Do You Feel Like We Do'?

is for **Q**ueen with Freddie's voice
and Brian's licks...

R

is for the **R**olling Stones and the blues of Keith and Mick.

is for **S**antana, and 'Samba Pa Ti'...

is for **T**om Petty, like a 'Refugee'.

U

is for the Velvet **U**nderground and 'Sweet Jane's inviting glance...

is for **V**an Morrison and his
marvelous 'Moondance'.

W

is for The **W**ho: Pete, Roger, Keith, and John...

is for T. Re**x**, 'Bang a Gong, Get it On'.

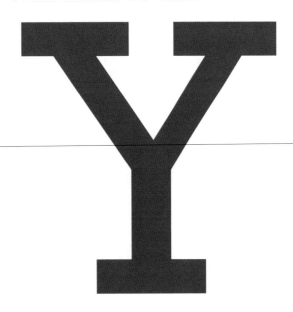

is for the **Y**ardbirds, three guitarists must be mentioned...

(Jeff Beck, Jimmy Page, and Eric Clapton)

is for Frank **Z**appa and the Mothers of Invention.

the
ROCK & ROLL ALPHABET

Rock and Roll can change your life,

it's rebellious, loud, and fun.

The music lasts forever

and your journey's just begun.

A picture's worth a thousand words,

or so it's often said.

These photographs speak volumes

through the pages you have read.

The show is never over,

and we hope you won't forget

to fill your life with music

like our Rocker's alphabet.